Designed by Flowerpot Press
in Franklin, TN.
www.FlowerpotPress.com
Designer: Jonas Fearon Bell
Editor: Hannah Lippard

CHC-0909-0035
ISBN: 978-1-4867-1293-9
Made in China
Fabrique en Chine

Guess How Much I Love Canada

Written by Katrine Crow
Illustrated by Mark Kummer

Whistler was the location for some of the 2010 Olympic and Paralympic sports.

Do you love Canada **THIS** much?

No! I love Canada more than that, because it has BRITISH COLUMBIA, where you can WHALE WATCH near VANCOUVER ISLAND, HIKE around GLACIER NATIONAL PARK, or go SKIING in WHISTLER! There are so many exciting places to visit, including the ROCKIES, the FAIRMONT EMPRESS in VICTORIA HARBOUR, BARKERVILLE, SCIENCE WORLD, and GRANVILLE ISLAND PUBLIC MARKET in VANCOUVER. But don't forget to try to catch a glimpse of a SPIRIT BEAR, a rare white Kermode bear that can only be found in GREAT BEAR RAINFOREST!

Barkerville is the largest historic site in western North America.

The Fairmont Empress serves over 500,000 cups of tea each year.

Canada broke the record for the most gold medals ever won at a single Winter Olympic Games in 2010. The Canadians claimed 14 gold medals that year.

Alberta

The West Edmonton Mall is the size of forty-eight city blocks.

Do you love Canada **THIS** much?

No! I love Canada more than that, because it has ALBERTA! You can visit BANFF NATIONAL PARK and hike around LAKE LOUISE, Canada's "hiking capital." Or you can take a trip to the WEST EDMONTON MALL, home of NORTH AMERICA'S largest indoor amusement park, where you can splash around at WORLD WATERPARK or visit GALAXYLAND! Take a trip to the ROYAL TYRRELL MUSEUM OF PALAEONTOLOGY to uncover cool DINOSAUR FOSSILS or check out the UFO LANDING PAD in ST. PAUL! But don't forget to grab your COWBOY BOOTS and stop by the RODEO at CALGARY STAMPEDE!

Lake Louise is the highest permanent settlement in Canada; it sits about 1,500 metres above sea level.

Calgary stampede attracts over one million attendees each year.

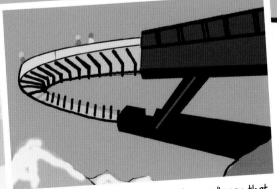

The Glacier Skywalk has a glass floor walkway that is about 280 metres above the ground!

Banff National Park is the oldest national park in Canada. The beautiful park was established in 1885.

No! I love Canada more than that, because it has **SASKATCHEWAN**! You can enjoy **VICTORIAN TEA** at the **GOVERNMENT HOUSE** in **REGINA**, take a hike through **PRINCE ALBERT NATIONAL PARK**, trek the **ATHABASCA SAND DUNES PROVINCIAL PARK**, spot wild plains bison in **GRASSLANDS NATIONAL PARK**, or walk the **SKYTRAIL BRIDGE**! But don't forget to stop by and say hello to **MEGAMUNCH**, the **ROBOTIC T. REX** at the **ROYAL SASKATCHEWAN MUSEUM**!

The Athabasca Sand Dunes are only accessible by boat or floatplane.

The Royal Saskatchewan Museum is home to Scotty, the most complete T. rex skeleton ever found.

Saskatchewan named curling its official sport in 2001. Many Saskatchewanians have won world championships and even Olympic medals in the sport!

No! I love Canada more than that, because it has three awesome territories: **NUNAVUT**, **NORTHWEST TERRITORIES**, and **YUKON**! There are so many beautiful landmarks and natural sites to visit, such as the **PENNY ICE CAP** in **AUYUITTUQ NATIONAL PARK**, the **NAHANNI NATIONAL PARK RESERVE** in **THE NORTHWEST TERRITORIES**, and **MILES CANYON**. You can also see the **TALLEST MOUNTAIN IN CANADA**, **MOUNT LOGAN**, and see **NARWHAL** in **POND INLET**, **NUNAVUT**. And make sure to stop by **SIGN POST FOREST**; it's one of the most famous landmarks along the **ALASKA HIGHWAY**!

The Prince of Wales Northern Heritage Centre opened in 1979.

Alert, Nunavut is one of the northernmost permanent settlements in the world. It's only 817 kilometres from the North Pole.

Mount Logan is named for Sir William Logan, founder of the Geological Survey of Canada. It's Canada's highest peak!

The Royal Canadian Mint can produce twenty million coins each day!

The Canadian Museum for Human Rights is the first national museum built outside of the National Capital Region in Ottawa.

Do you love Canada **THIS** much?

The Narcisse Snake Dens is the largest gathering of snakes in the world.

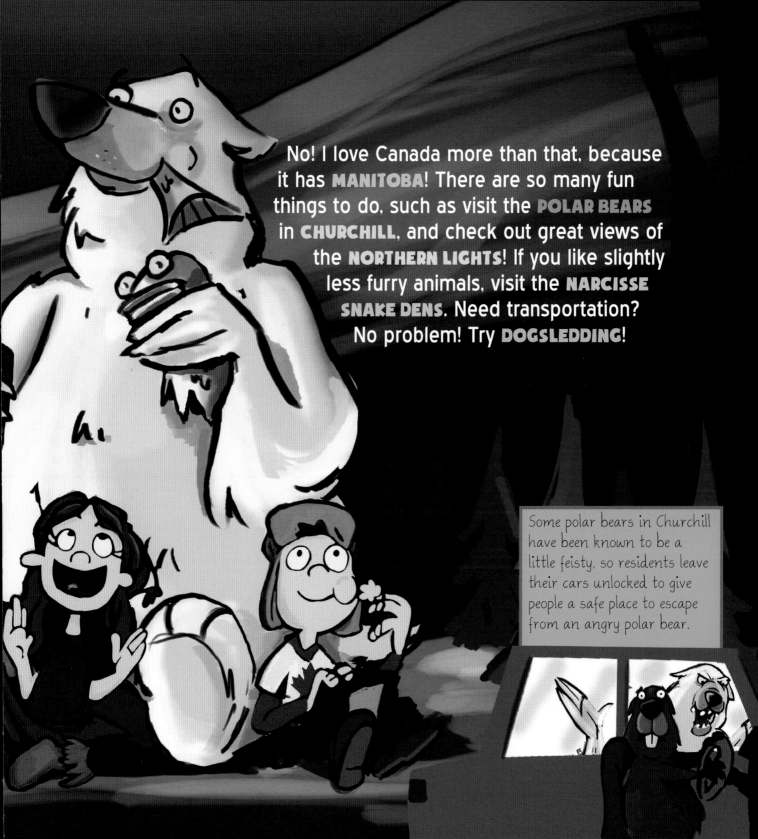

No! I love Canada more than that, because it has **MANITOBA**! There are so many fun things to do, such as visit the **POLAR BEARS** in **CHURCHILL**, and check out great views of the **NORTHERN LIGHTS**! If you like slightly less furry animals, visit the **NARCISSE SNAKE DENS**. Need transportation? No problem! Try **DOGSLEDDING**!

Some polar bears in Churchill have been known to be a little feisty, so residents leave their cars unlocked to give people a safe place to escape from an angry polar bear.

Canada's Wonderland is home to one of the tallest and fastest roller coasters in the world, Leviathan.

The CN Tower is struck by lightning on average seventy-five times per year.

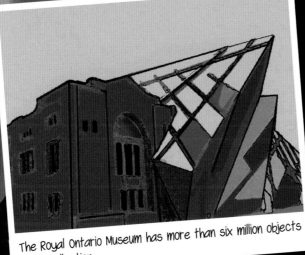

The Royal Ontario Museum has more than six million objects in its collection.

No! I love Canada more than that, because it has **ONTARIO**, where you can visit beautiful **NIAGARA FALLS** and go to the top of the **CN TOWER**. There are also other amazing sites to visit, such as **PARLIAMENT HILL** in **OTTAWA**, the **ROYAL ONTARIO MUSEUM**, and the **HOCKEY HALL OF FAME**. And while you're there, you should ride a roller coaster at **CANADA'S WONDERLAND**!

No! I love Canada more than that, because it has **QUÉBEC**! You can stroll the streets of **OLD MONTRÉAL**, marvel at the **CHÂTEAU FRONTENAC** and the **NOTRE-DAME BASILICA**, or stay the night in the **HÔTEL DE GLACE** (don't forget your warm winter coat)! Best of all, you can try some delicious **POUTINE**— it's a Canadian favourite made of french fries topped with cheese curds and gravy! Yum!!

The Notre-Dame Basilica only took thirty-five months to build.

Château Frontenac is considered the world's most photographed hotel.

HELLO

BONJOUR

French and English are both official languages of Canada. Most of Canada's French-speaking population lives in Québec.

New Brunswick

Do you love Canada **THIS** much?

No! I love Canada more than that, because it has **NEW BRUNSWICK**, where you can hike through the beautiful **FUNDY NATIONAL PARK**, check out the **HOPEWELL ROCKS**, and shop the **SAINT JOHN CITY MARKET**. Don't visit without seeing the **WORLD'S LARGEST LOBSTER STATUE** in **SHEDIAC**, the "lobster capital of the world!"

More types of whales can be found more often in the Bay of Fundy than anywhere else in the world!

The Confederation Bridge is about thirteen kilometres long.

The Hopewell Rocks are also called the Flowerpot Rocks.

Nova Scotia

Do you love Canada **THIS** much?

Canada is a constitutional monarchy ruled by Queen Elizabeth II. She is both the Queen of Canada and Canada's Head of State.

No! I love Canada more than that, because it has **NOVA SCOTIA**, where you can visit the **ALEXANDER GRAHAM BELL NATIONAL HISTORIC SITE**, the famous **BIG FIDDLE**, and the historic **FORTRESS OF LOUISBOURG**! **NOVA SCOTIA** is also home to the **FUNDY GEOLOGICAL MUSEUM** in Parrsboro, where you can check out awesome **DINOSAUR FOSSILS**. It even has the largest number of lighthouses in Canada, including **PEGGY'S COVE LIGHTHOUSE**!

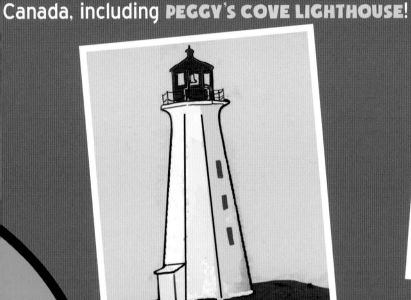

Peggy's Cove Lighthouse has been standing on the shores of Nova Scotia since 1915.

The Big Fiddle in Sydney is just over eighteen metres tall.

The Alexander Graham Bell National Historic Site is the home of many of Bell's artifacts and personal belongings.

Prince Edward Island

Do you love Canada **THIS** much?

The Point Prim Lighthouse is the island's oldest lighthouse.

Canada's motto is "A Mari Usque Ad Mare," which means "From Sea To Sea."

No! I love Canada more than that, because it has **PRINCE EDWARD ISLAND**! You can visit the GREEN GABLES HOUSE and PORT-LA-JOYE-FORT AMHERST, ride your bike on CONFEDERATION TRAIL, or stroll along the beach in **BASIN HEAD PROVINCIAL PARK**! The oldest lighthouse on the island is at POINT PRIM, where you can sit by the sea and eat the best SEAFOOD at THE CHOWDER HOUSE!

The Green Gables House is the home that inspired the classic Anne of Green Gables books.

Port-la-Joye—Fort Amherst was named a National Historic Site of Canada in 1958.

No! I love Canada more than that, because it has **NEWFOUNDLAND AND LABRADOR**! You can visit the colourful city of **ST. JOHN'S**, both **TERRA NOVA** and **GROS MORNE NATIONAL PARKS**, and the **CAPE SPEAR LIGHTHOUSE**. If you like history, you should check out **CABOT TOWER** on **SIGNAL HILL** and **L'ANSE AUX MEADOWS NATIONAL HISTORIC SITE**. If you prefer a little more excitement, go to **BONAVISTA PENINSULA** to see adorable **PUFFINS**!

The Cape Spear Lighthouse marks the easternmost point of North America.

Cabot Tower is the site of the first-ever received transatlantic transmission.

YES!
I love Canada that much because it is **AWESOME**, and has all this **COOL** stuff, and I think it might be my **FAVOURITE PLACE EVER**!